Useful Not True

USEFUL NOT TRUE

DEREK SIVERS

HIT MEDIA

Copyright © 2024 by Sivers Inc
All rights reserved

Producer: Saeah Lee Wood

Useful Not True ISBNs:
978-0-47-345303-9 hardcover
978-0-47-345304-6 paperback
978-0-47-345305-3 ebook
978-0-47-345306-0 audiobook

Go to **sive.rs** for quantity sales, special discounts, and custom dedications directly from the author.

Hit Media
Oxford, Shanghai, Bangalore, Dubai
hitmedia.com

Contents

Before

What's this about?   2

Almost Nothing People Say Is True

What time is it?   4
Perspectives feel real   5
No picture is the whole picture   6
People share perspectives, not facts   7
Separate events and interpretation   8
Bridge guard   10
Rules are a starting point, not the final answer   12
Obligations are not true   14
Cultural meanings   15
Try to find their incentives   17
The brain invents explanations   18
Memories are not accurate   20
The past is not true   21
Wanna bet?   23
Even science isn't true   24

Fake or real? True or false? So what?	25
Bridge guard, revisited	26
That was about you, not them	27

Your Thoughts Aren't True

You are the strange one	29
You can't trust your mind	30
Re-edit your mind's movies	31
Hanging inherited paintings	33
Make believe	34
Beliefs are not facts	36
The more emotional the belief, the less likely it's true	37
Your first thought is an obstacle	38
Fill your senses with reality	40

Ideas Can Be Useful, Not True

Bowling: curve into the target	42
A daily run and imagination	43
Beliefs → emotions → actions	44
Useful?	45
Religion is action, not belief	46
Carpenters' tools	48
Judge the contents, not the box	49
Which perspective empowers you?	50
Magic mirror shows what you need to believe	51

Placebo meanings	52
Life is _____	53
What is "the truth" really for?	56
Philosophies are instruments	57

Reframe: Find Better Perspectives

The most useful part of this book	60
Who chooses your (next) thoughts?	61
Answer great questions	62
Diamond in the trash	63
Expand your repertoire	64
Traits of useful perspectives	65
Five tiny tales of reframing	67
An awesome collection of great questions	69

Adopt What Works For You Now

How to decide and make the best choice	71
From explorer to self-leader	72
No new instructions for the computer	73
Private journal to internalize it	74
Talk with friends to solidify it	75
Why your choice is wrong	76
Take the first step immediately	77
Keep tuning and adjusting	78
You are what you pretend to be	79

After

Reframing death 81
What next? 82
More books on this subject 83
Books by Derek Sivers 88

Before

What's this about?

This book is about reframing — changing how you think about something — and choosing a perspective that's useful to you right now, whether or not it's universally true.

Before we begin, I need to sharpen that word: "true". **In this book, when I say "true", I mean absolutely, necessarily, objectively true.** It's not only in the mind. Any creature or machine could observe it and agree. It's a concrete fact — always, everywhere, and for everyone. There's no other way to see it. That's what I mean by "true".

This narrow definition is important because whatever you consider true is closed. No questioning. But when you say "not *necessarily* true", it opens it up for reconsideration.

Notice that "not true" does not mean false! It just means not necessarily, objectively, absolutely true for everyone, everywhere, always. It doesn't mean you're wrong. It means there could be another possibility or perspective.

Let's look at "Useful Not True" in five steps:

1. Almost nothing people say is true.
2. Your thoughts aren't true.
3. Ideas can be useful, not true.
4. Reframe: Find better perspectives.
5. Adopt what works for you now.

Almost Nothing People Say Is True

What time is it?

"What time is it right now?"

For who? You? For most people in the world, that's not the current time.

"What day is it today?"

For who? You? I'm in New Zealand, so it's Saturday. For my friends in America, it's Friday.

In Fiji, I went to the island of Taveuni. That's where the international date line crosses. There's a sign and a line on the ground. You can step back and forth across it. Left foot, Sunday. Right foot, Monday. It reminds you that dates are subjective. But your feet are in the sand, and that's true.

"When does summer begin?"

For who? You? For half the planet, Christmas is summer and July is winter.

This is a silly but important reminder. People speak as if they're stating facts. They say things like "You can't do that" and "Here's what women want". **But it's just their current perspective.** It's their metaphorical time zone, which is probably different from yours.

They're not *wrong*. It's just not the only answer.

Perspectives feel real

A kid says a cat is a pet. A mouse says a cat is a threat. They can't see it any other way. Their friends agree, which solidifies their view, making it feel totally true.

"This house is overpriced."

"Nothing matters more than family."

"You're talking too much."

To the person speaking, these feel like facts, not opinions. They really think that house is overpriced, and you're talking too much. But someone is happy to buy that house at that price, and someone wants you to talk more, so their statements are not necessarily true.

Someone says, "That behavior is immoral and wrong." But from another perspective, that behavior is moral and right. So, essentially, the person is just saying, "I don't like it."

Every statement everyone says could be prefaced with a disclaimer: **"From my limited point of view, based only on what I've experienced…"**

But they don't need to say that. Instead, we need to know that, and hear it that way. No matter how much authority or conviction they have, no matter how respected or famous they are, their statements are just one biased point of view.

No picture is the whole picture

They say the camera never lies. But of course it does.

Someone shows you photos of happy people laughing. They say this is proof that people are doing well.

Someone else shows you photos of people looking sad. They say this is proof that people are miserable.

Ironically, all the photos were taken at the same place and the same time. But one camera focused on the happiness, while the other focused on the misery.

Both claim that their photos show the truth. But it's just one perspective.

People find facts to support their argument on any debatable topic or view of the world. **Facts can be true, while the perspective is not.**

No picture is the whole picture. It's just one of many possible angles.

People share perspectives, not facts

People communicate for social and emotional reasons. (Notice the word "commune" in "communicate".)

Socially, they want to bond. Judgements, gossip, ethics, and opinions are all great for signaling and connecting.

Emotionally, they want validation. They want others to acknowledge and agree that their viewpoint is justified. When you can see someone's point of view, it tells them that you're standing on their side.

That's why people rarely share objective unbiased facts. Actual facts are as boring as dirt. **Nobody bonds over facts.** They have more incentive to share their thoughts, which are never necessarily true.

Separate events and interpretation

A young man in a hooded sweatshirt knocks at your door, hiding his face, looking nervously around. "Hey, hey, yeah, can I come in? I, uh, need a glass of water." You say no, and don't let him in.

A well-dressed old lady knocks at your door. "I'm so sorry, my dear, but I was walking home and started feeling faint. Could I trouble you for a glass of water?" You say yes of course, let her in, and get her a glass of water. After she thanks you and leaves, you notice your wallet is gone.

Language can be sneaky like this. Some statements are clearly suspicious, so you don't let them pass. Others sound trustworthy, so you let them in with your defenses down. But their hidden judgements will steal your clarity if you don't stop them at the door.

Your friend says, "My mother abandoned me." Stop. Get the actual facts. Turns out his mother had two full-time jobs, so he was raised by his grandmother in the same town, and stayed with his mother on weekends. So he's really saying that he *felt* abandoned. It helps both of you distinguish between the facts and the feelings.

Another friend says someone is needy, stubborn, and inappropriate, as if those are traits. But the person judging is usually just expressing their unmet expectations. So the statement tells you more about the accuser, and almost nothing about the accused.

Imagine the job of a police clerk, filing an incident report by listening to all the emotionally charged accusations to record the few, unbiased, observable events.

Feelings matter. To address them, we have to distinguish them. **Get the dry facts, with no interpretation. What's left are the feelings and meanings.** We can't change what happened, but we can change the meaning we give it, which changes how we feel about it.

Bridge guard

A group of adventurers needed to cross the narrow bridge over the deadly canyon. But a huge threatening guard — like the genie from Aladdin's lamp — blocked the entrance. He said, in a booming voice, "No one can cross until you tell me what's true!"

He snapped his fingers, and everyone's vision was replaced with a scene. The king, presented with a bowl of soup, took a sip, then pushed it away with a scowl saying, "It's too salty." Then their vision returned.

An adventurer said, "The king doesn't like the soup?"

The guard boomed, "NO!"

"He thinks it's too salty?"

"NO!"

Then one said, "He said the words: 'It's too salty.'"

"TRUE!"

That one person was allowed to cross the bridge.

Then, blocking again, "No one can cross until you tell me what's true!"

He snapped his fingers and they saw a new scene. A woman is trapped in a box and can't get out. She's pushing, pounding, and trying everything, but nothing is working. Then their vision returned.

"She's trapped in a box and can't get out?"

"NO!"

"She's trying everything, but nothing is working?"

"NO!"

Then one said, "She's pushing and pounding the box?"

"TRUE!"

That one person was allowed to cross the bridge.

Then, blocking again, "No one can cross until …"

But the youngest girl in the group figured it out. She walked right up to the fearsome bridge guard and said, "I'm going to cross now." Then she squeezed past his legs and crossed the bridge. So the rest did the same.

The guard smiled with pride.

Rules are a starting point, not the final answer

Kids make up rules for games.

"Got you!"

"No, I was still touching the base, remember?"

"Well I've got the talisman in my pocket so that doesn't count."

"Fine, but from now on you can only use that once per game."

"OK, but no tag-backs for five seconds."

Instead of playing by the rules, they're playing *with* the rules — playing with the game itself. **Changing the game is part of the fun.** We can still do this.

Rules set expectations and the terms of the game. They're a useful starting point, but they're not the final answer.

Governments and businesses make rules, but those rules are as random as children's games, created by a similar process. A few people in an office, tired and wanting to break for lunch, agreed on something and haven't thought of it since. An assistant typed it into an official document. The person enforcing it just learned about it last week, and doesn't really care, but doesn't want to get in trouble. *They* treat these rules as true because it makes their job easier. But they're negotiable.

Rules can be ignored. Breaking a rule can be rational and moral, if you understand the rule's purpose, and no one is harmed.

My friend was part of a student protest in Chicago thirty-five years ago, when he was eighteen, and was arrested for a few hours. Thirty years later, he and his wife went for a vacation in Australia. Upon arrival, the visa forms ask if you've ever been arrested. He ticked "yes". The border control guy at the airport wouldn't let him in the country and sent them back on the next flight to Chicago. They were devastated. Thousands of dollars lost. Vacation ruined. Before they left, the officer said, "Next time, make it easier for everyone. Just tick 'no'."

Rules can be changed. Society doesn't want rules to change, since most people don't want the trouble. But improving the rules over time is necessary. Someone has to do it.

When the founding fathers of the United States of America were drafting the constitution, it was assumed this new country would have three, six, or twelve presidents. When someone proposed having only one president, most delegates were against it, since they had just left a kingdom, and wanted nothing like a king. The issue was debated for weeks before finally agreeing, by a 7-to-3 vote, to have just one president. It's a reminder that the way things are is arbitrary, and not the only way.

The world is as negotiable as a flea market in Marrakesh. Only a fool doesn't haggle.

Obligations are not true

Family, friends, colleagues, and communities put social pressure on you to do what they want you to do. They say it's your obligation or your duty. But those terms are social expectations. They're not real. They're not even universal. They're just one way to see the situation.

The people saying it's your obligation really just want you to do something. But instead of saying "I want," they blame a higher legitimacy. It's manipulative. They say their wishes are laws you must obey. But if they didn't personally want you to do it, they would have said, "Don't worry about it."

Some people say their feelings are your problem. But that's ridiculous. You can't control people's feelings. They *are* able to choose their response. (The word "responsible" comes from response-able.)

Everyone has their own problems. To know whose problem it is, think who benefits most from solving it.

The boss says you need to work late. But that indicates a flaw in the company's system, which is their problem, not yours. Maybe working late would ultimately harm the company by keeping them from finding a more sustainable solution.

Parents say, "You need to take care of us when we're old." But maybe we all need to prepare for our own future care instead of burdening others with it.

They might say you're a bad person for not doing what they want you to do. But that's not true. Maybe they're just disappointed that you're not taking their wish as your command.

Cultural meanings

One of my best friends from Singapore was visiting me here in New Zealand last summer. She and I were upstairs when a local friend of mine came by and yelled from downstairs, "Yo D!" I yelled down, "We're upstairs!" He let himself in, helped himself to a drink in the fridge, came up barefoot and sweaty, and laid down on the floor.

My Singaporean friend told me later this was really confusing, since the way this guy and I were acting towards each other was so rude. In her culture, all guests are treated with hospitality. But to me, that would feel off-putting, treating a dear friend like a formal acquaintance. To me, casual familiarity is the most endearing. Mi casa, su casa.

Actions have no inherent meaning. To yell "come in" instead of answering the door can be offensive to one person and endearing to another. **When someone tells you what something means, it's never true because it's not the only answer.** It's just one perspective. You might do something you think is polite, only to have someone tell you it's rude.

A British woman moved to China and lived with a Chinese family for a year. She ate dinner with her host family every night, and became conversationally fluent in Mandarin.

One night, after she asked, "Could you please pass the salt?" her host mother scolded her, saying, "You're being rude."

The British woman was confused and said, "I'm sorry. I said 'please'."

The mother said, "Listen to us. We're family. When we

want salt, we just say 'salt!' You're part of our family, too. Using formal manners here in our home is rude because it treats us like strangers."

Manners, norms, and meanings are never true. This is important to remember when people tell you this is good, that is bad, this means that, etc.

Try to find their incentives

Middle of the night. You're fast asleep. You hear a loud "BANG!" downstairs. Your body kicks into emergency danger mode. Eventually you find out that your cat knocked over the broom. Mystery solved. Back to sleep.

You're trying to enjoy a quiet day at the park, but this annoying little girl won't stop screaming. You leave the park, angry at a stranger. On your way out, you see the girl has been screaming in pain because she fell out of a tree and her leg is clearly broken. Your anger is replaced with sympathy.

These two stories are similar. When something is confusing, alarming, or unexplained, we assume the worst. But once it's explained, we relax.

When we don't understand someone, they feel like an outsider — maybe subconsciously an enemy. It's primal and tribal to feel defensive. Our ancestors had reason to be wary, and survived by being suspicious. But once we learn the reason, cause, or origin of someone's behavior or belief, we can start to feel empathy and connection.

When someone believes something that seems crazy to you, **consider what incentives, from their point of view, make that belief useful**. It helps you understand someone, and helps you feel less defensive. It helps you separate the person and the actions — to see their beliefs not as who they are, but as something they're currently holding for a purpose.

The brain invents explanations

Some people have damaged fibers connecting the left and right hemispheres of their brain, and need to have that connection surgically severed. They live pretty normal lives even though the two sides of their brain are disconnected. Psychologists work with these people to better understand the brain.

They showed a patient a message to her right eye, saying, "Please close the window." She got up and closed the window.

Then they showed a question to her left eye, "Why did you close the window?" She said she chose to do it because she was cold.

To another patient, a researcher said, to only one ear, "Please walk." The patient started walking.

Then they asked his other ear, "Why did you walk?" He said he just felt like getting a drink.

One woman being tested for seizures had electrodes implanted in her brain. When they stimulated one area, she started laughing hysterically. The doctors asked why. She said the picture on the wall is really funny. Later, when probing that same area again, while she was eating, she laughed again. This time, she said it's because her fork is really funny.

These people weren't lying. They fully believed those were the real reasons.

This isn't just brain patients. It's an insight into the human condition: something that everyone does all the time, but these tests were able to show. **When asked for**

an explanation, the brain invents a reason and completely believes it. To that person, the explanation feels like absolute fact — the kind they swear is true, believe deeply in their core, and will fight to defend!

Think of the implications: major life choices, attraction, excitement, love, jealousy, revenge, anxiety, fear, and interpersonal conflict. All of these are supported and defended by explanations that aren't true.

People's motives are unknowable, even to themselves. Let go of the need for a reason. Ignore their explanations. The only true facts are their actions.

Memories are not accurate

January 28, 1986, at 11:39am, the Space Shuttle exploded during liftoff, killing all seven crew members. It was a big deal. As soon as it happened, everyone stopped what they were doing to watch the TV updates.

Because it was a school day in America, a psychology professor handed out a questionnaire to his freshman students, asking what they had been doing moments earlier when they had first heard the news. Where were you? Who were you with? What were you doing?

Then, he saved their answers for three years, for the sake of what came next.

Three years later, he gave those same students the same questionnaire, asking what they had been doing when the Space Shuttle exploded. After they answered, he asked how confident they were in their answers. Almost all of them said 100%.

Then he showed them their original answers from the day it happened. **Nobody remembered correctly.** Their answers were all different. Everybody had misremembered their own facts.

Memories feel like facts, but they're not. People don't doubt their memory, but you should.

The past is not true

When I was 17, I was driving recklessly and crashed into an oncoming car. I found out that I broke the other driver's spine, and she'll never walk again.

I carried that burden with me everywhere, and felt so horrible about it for so many years that at age 35 I decided to find this woman to apologize. I found her name and address, went to her house, knocked on the door, and a middle-aged woman answered. As soon as I said, "I'm the teenager that hit your car eighteen years ago and broke your spine," I started sobbing — a big ugly cry, surfacing years of regret. She was so sweet, and hugged me saying, "Oh sweetie, sweetie! Don't worry. I'm fine!" Then she walked me into her living room. Walked.

Turns out I had misunderstood. Yes she fractured a couple vertebrae but it never stopped her from walking. She said "that little accident" helped her pay more attention to her fitness, and since then has been taking better care of her health. Then she apologized for causing the accident in the first place. Apologized.

I said, "Well, no, it was my fault for ignoring the yield sign."

She said, "No, it was my fault because I was eating while driving and not watching the road. You didn't hit me. I hit you."

Seems we had both thought the accident was our fault, and had spent eighteen years feeling bad about it. This time, she started crying and said, "It's so *stupid* — these stories."

Aim a laser pointer at the moon, then move your hand the tiniest bit, and it'll move a thousand miles at the other end.

The tiniest misunderstanding long ago, amplified through time, leads to giant misunderstandings in the present.

We think of the past like it's a physical fact — like it's real. But we never have all the information — only interpretation. **One story based on one point of view: that's what we call *"the* past".**

Wanna bet?

By definition, "the future" doesn't exist. It's what we call predictions in our imagination.

People think that the more vivid the image is in their mind, the more likely it's real. They say, "I'm sure it's going to happen. I can feel it. I can picture it now."

People are so certain about their predictions.

"This meeting is going to be so boring."

"More funding will help."

"If that guy gets elected, it'll be a disaster."

"I'd be happier with a bigger house."

None of those statements are true, because nobody knows the future. We can't even predict our own reactions. Winning the lottery or having an accident might be surprisingly bad or good. Even a statement as simple as "I need to relax" might not be true, since it's a prediction that relaxing will help. **The problem is certainty, and not realizing it's a prediction.**

Try asking, "How much do you want to bet?"

Or maybe, "How confident are you about that prediction, from 0 to 100%?"

Instead of black or white, right or wrong, it will probably be degrees, like "80% sure".

When they realize their confidence is less than 100%, they can consider other possibilities.

Even science isn't true

When I started writing this book, my friend asked me for an example of what I consider to be true. I said science. He's a scientist, so he got a good long laugh and said, "No no no! Science is useful, but not true!" Then he explained.

In the scientific process, nothing is final or complete. No model is "true". Each one just aims to be less and less wrong. **Every conclusion is an invitation to improve it.** Scientists learn about existing findings, question them, and try to supersede them. It's better to be curious than correct. It's intellectual humility.

Newton's laws of motion from the 1600s work for most situations. Then Albert Einstein developed the theory of relativity, which showed that Newton's laws aren't sufficient. Then quantum mechanics showed limitations in Einstein's theory. But yet, to land on the moon, or launch a satellite into orbit, we still use Newton's laws since they're simple and good enough for that purpose.

The most accurate theory is not always the most useful. And a rule of thumb can be far from true, but good enough to get you where you need to go.

Fake or real? True or false? So what?

People have always made up nonsense, and made others believe it. That's nothing new. But now computers create text that sounds human and video that looks real.

Cultures of the world have always had conflicting values, but they used to be isolated. Everyone around you agreed on what's right and wrong, and how to live. But now everyone is connected, so these clashing values are confusing or enraging.

It helps to see almost nothing as necessarily true.

Saying "So what?" sounds dismissive, but it's asking an important question: **"So what are you going to *do* about it?"**

You see a video of an important person saying something shocking. Is it taken out of context? Is it fake and actually generated by a computer?

You argue with someone who has different beliefs. They say your values are harmful and wrong.

The news is reporting something upsetting. Is it falsified propaganda or misrepresentation?

If it's true, what would you do? If it's false, what would you do? Consider both scenarios and figure out your response.

You might never know the absolute truth, so what matters are *your* actions. **If belief or doubt makes you do something good, then choose that view because it's useful to you.** If you'll do nothing, either way, then never mind.

Bridge guard, revisited

I want to make sure the point of the "Bridge guard" story came across.

The king said, "It's too salty." Did he actually think it's too salty? Who knows? Maybe he doesn't want to admit that he's tired or sick. Maybe he's testing the chef's confidence. Just because someone says something doesn't mean it's true.

The woman in the box is pushing and pounding. But we shouldn't jump to the conclusion that she's "trapped, can't get out, trying everything, and nothing is working". That's the kind of self-defeating belief we're surrounded with in everyday life.

The girl put these two examples together, and got the message that the guard isn't actually blocking the bridge. Just because he says "no one can cross" doesn't mean it's true.

That's what this part of the book was about. Distrust limitations. Strip away interpretations to see the few actual facts. **We're held back not by raw facts, but by the meanings we give them.**

That was about you, not them

All of the chapters until now have been about other people. It's so easy to see their faults. So full of nonsense, thinking they're so right, with their weird beliefs. It's much harder to find fault in yourself.

Only after I see mistakes in others do I realize that I make those same mistakes. That's why I put the chapters in this order. First I pointed at other people, so you could clearly see their faulty thinking. Now let's remember that you make those same mistakes.

- Almost nothing you say is true.
- You focus on one angle of the whole picture.
- Your brain makes up explanations.
- Your perspective feels like a fact.
- Your certain future is just a prediction.
- Your thoughts are theories, open for improvement.

Consider what incentives made *your* beliefs useful.

This book, start to finish, is entirely about you. Maybe you're full of nonsense, thinking you're so right, thinking your beliefs are actually true.

Your Thoughts Aren't True

You are the strange one

A traveler comes to a river and sees a local woman on the opposite bank. He yells across, "How do I get to the other side of the river?"

She yells back, "You *are* on the other side of the river!"

An American woman went on a vacation to Scotland. Talking with a group of people there, she said, "I just love your accent!"

They said, "We don't have an accent. You do."

For hundreds of years, people worshipped Zeus, Athena, Odin, and Thor. Now we call it mythology. But when it comes to our own beliefs? No no no! Those are just true! Only *others'* beliefs are myths and superstitions.

You take some principles or values very seriously. You think of them as undeniable truths. But to other people, you are the one with silly beliefs.

See yourself from the other side of the river. You have an accent. **Since you know other people's beliefs aren't true, you have to realize that yours are also not true.**

You can't trust your mind

There was a crime out on Park Avenue today, so the police are gathering information. A helpful witness said, "He had a red mustache, green eyes, and a scar by his right ear. He was 6-foot-1 and had a tattoo of a dragon on his right shoulder." The police said, "This is great information. How sure are you of this?" The witness said, "I'm completely sure. 100% positive. I mean, I didn't see it first-hand because I was inside the back room with no windows, but I think I heard someone whispering something like this."

That's your brain, in the dark, inside your skull. It can't see or hear, or experience anything directly. It interprets little signals sent through nerves, which is not much information to work with, so it's often mistaken. But it tells you it's completely sure. 100% positive.

The movies that scare me the most are the ones where the hero realizes he can't trust his own mind. "Vanilla Sky", "Memento", "A Beautiful Mind", "Jacob's Ladder", "The Others", "Fight Club", "The Sixth Sense", and "The Matrix". It's terrifying to find out you're crazy. What you thought was real is not. **But if you can't trust your mind, what can you do?**

In each of these movies, the hero gets through it for the better. When he finds out his mind has been tricking him, it's upsetting, but he adapts. His mind was at odds with reality but can now see the difference. It's even a relief, because it explains some frustrating moments of confusion in his past. Since old beliefs were disproven, the hero takes in reality with clear eyes. He carefully proceeds with less confidence and more humility. So can you.

Re-edit your mind's movies

The movie "500 Days of Summer" is a beautiful example of doubting your past. We see many scenes of a boy and a girl happily in love, but always from his point of view.

Then suddenly, the girl says, "I think we should stop seeing each other."

The boy is shocked and confused, and sinks into depression because he's convinced that she's his true love, and he doesn't understand why she would break up, since they were so happy.

Eventually, his little sister says, "I think you're just remembering the good stuff. Next time you look back, you should look again."

Then the movie does something wonderful. **It replays those same scenes it showed before, but now with a different edit.**

Before, we saw her smile at him, but now the camera watches longer, and we see her smile was fake, lasting only a second. Now we see they had many fights.

Before, we saw them holding hands, but now we see he tried to hold her hand and she refused it, pulling away. Now we see that she never loved him.

The signs were there all along.

He had been focusing only on the happy memories, ignoring the rest. When he focuses on the bad memories, her breakup is not confusing or even painful. This perspective helps him **make peace with the past** and move on.

Consider this cinematic approach for the memories that haunt you.

For example: almost everyone says they were unpopular in school — that they were bullied and teased. They form their self-identity around that story. "People make fun of me. I'm not one of those likeable, popular types."

It's probably not true. It's probably a misinterpretation — not realizing that happened to everyone.

Next time you look back, look again. Replay your past from different angles until you find the lesson or closure you need.

Hanging inherited paintings

My mom inherited an ugly painting from her mom. It hung in the living room, and visitors would comment on how it felt wrong. But she kept it there for sentimental reasons.

One day, when she took it out to be reframed, they found the artist's signature and date written underneath the old frame. Turns out the painting had been hanging upside-down this whole time. Turned right-side-up, it looked much better.

Kind of like beliefs. **We inherit pictures of how to think and act, and tend to keep them as-is, even if they're problematic.**

Your mother always said, "be careful", teaching you to live in fear. Your father had a terrible temper, teaching you to not share your thoughts. Your first major breakup taught you that you don't deserve love.

This is the interior design of your mind — your internal environment. Take these paintings out under a bright light to be reframed. When you remove the frame and flip them upside-down, you can make sure they're hanging the right way. Or decide to throw them away.

Make believe

Kids scream, "Monster in the hallway!", and hide behind the couch. They stack up cushions for protection, and plan their defense.

They know there's not *really* a monster in the hallway, but it's exciting to feel the adrenaline of panic, to make a shelter and feel safe.

One kid yells, "The floor is hot lava!" Leaping between furniture is a fun challenge.

One slips and wails, "Help! I'm falling! Save me! Save me!" Now one kid can feel protected, while the other gets to be the rescuing hero.

Mom calls, "Pancakes are ready!", and all stories stop when the kids run into the kitchen.

Kids believe anything fun for a while. It's called "make believe" because they're making up beliefs.

The game has a purpose. Each belief gives them a new situation, and lets them adopt a new role like protector or inventor.

Grown-ups have their own version of make believe:

"Everything happens for a reason."

"Those people are evil."

"I would be creatively prolific if I could quit my job."

None of these statements are true. But we like the way it feels to believe.

Beliefs have a purpose. They help us adopt a perspective or identity. They help us take action, or cooperate with others.

The only problem is when we confuse belief with reality, and insist that something is absolutely true because we believe it.

Beliefs don't exist outside the mind. (Have you ever seen one in nature?) All beliefs are make believe.

Beliefs are not facts

Whenever someone says, "I believe …", then whatever they say next is not true. If it was a fact, there would be no need to declare a belief.

You don't say, "I believe in squirrels." You don't say, "I believe squares have four sides." It's just a fact, so there's no need to take a stance.

You say "I believe" when it's not a fact that everyone can see. Since people view it differently, you share *your* perspective on how *you* see it.

A belief is something you think is true, without proof. A fact is an objective reality — something proven true — verified with conclusive evidence.

No beliefs are true. If a belief was proven true, it would no longer be a belief.

Galileo believed the planets orbit around the sun, but he didn't have proof. Hundreds of years later, when it was proven true, it ceased to be a belief and became a fact. But in his lifetime, it was just a belief.

Beliefs are a stance on what's inconclusive. **You have to say "I believe …" because it's not the only answer.** It's not a fact. (Not yet.)

The more emotional the belief, the less likely it's true

Some beliefs are basically facts, but without absolute proof. Tomatoes are a vegetable. Tonight's movie starts at 7:00. Then my friend shows me proof that tomatoes are a fruit and the movie starts at 8:00. Cool! I'm glad to be corrected.

Some beliefs make people really emotional. Think of one of your particularly strong beliefs. If someone showed you *absolute proof* that your belief is wrong, would you be glad to be corrected? Would you instantly change your mind? Why not? Maybe you see that belief as a part of who you are? Would changing it change your public persona? Your self-identity?

Some people, when challenged on their beliefs, get all upset and scream, "But I believe this deeply in my heart of hearts!"

Wow, look at all that emotion! It must actually be true! Yeah, right. As if the amount of emotion measures the truth of the belief. Maybe it measures the opposite. **If it was absolutely objectively true, there would be no need to get upset. You could just point to the conclusive proof.** That's that.

Instead, you might be using that word "believe" to mean "my identity depends on this". Especially if you feel the need to tell everyone your beliefs.

Your first thought is an obstacle

Here's a common optical illusion:

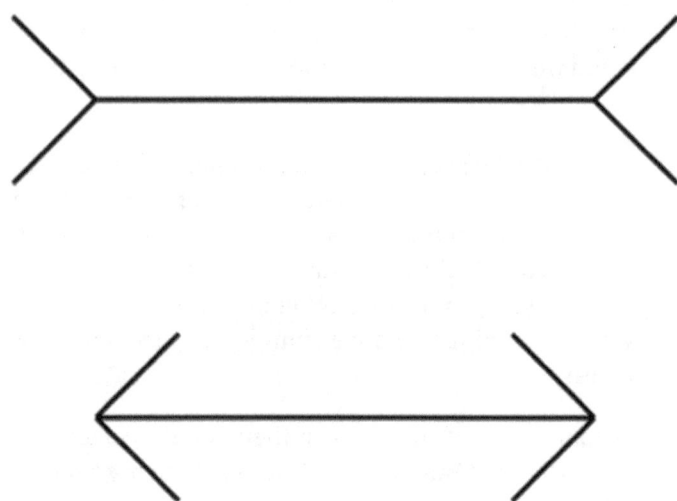

Two horizontal lines, the same length. The top one has diagonal lines going *out* from its edges. The bottom one has diagonal lines going *in* from its edges.

Your instincts insist that the top line is obviously longer. But if you measure them to confirm, you'll prove to yourself they're actually the same.

So **your wisdom has to go against your instincts**, and remind yourself the lines are actually the same, **even though it feels wrong.** You override your instincts with wisdom.

Your instinct says somebody wronged you. Your wisdom reminds you that they could say the same about you.

Your instinct says your current situation is horrible and hopeless. Your wisdom reminds you that you can use any situation to your advantage.

Your instinct says you know right from wrong. Your wisdom reminds you that your norms are one of many valid perspectives.

Your first thought is an obstacle. **You need to get past it.** Outsmart it.

Your instinct never goes away. But let your wisdom have the final say.

Fill your senses with reality

When I'm feeling troubled, it helps to look around at reality. Am I in physical danger? No. I'm in a room. I'm safe. It's a reminder that the trouble is in my head.

So I get away from all people and media, to avoid all viewpoints, opinions, and drama. I shut off my devices. I go to a place where the natural world is untouched by humans. Ideally deep into nature and stay a few days, but a beach or a forest for an hour will do.

I fill my senses with reality: wind blowing, waves crashing, plants and animals doing their thing. This place was about the same a million years ago, and a million years from now, when people are gone. Nature carries on. Humans are just another chattering species, making noise like birds and dogs.

Almost nothing people say is true. My thoughts aren't true. Norms, obligations, the past, the future, and fears: none of it is real. They're just thoughts formed into stories. Out here, they don't exist.

I find this a better starting place for reframing.

Ideas Can Be Useful, Not True

Bowling: curve into the target

I'm pretty bad at bowling and frisbee. I roll the ball or throw the disc straight at the target, but away it curves. After this happens a few times, I adjust. I stop aiming straight since that's not working. If it always curves to the left, I aim to the right.

It feels wrong to aim away from the target. But it curves back to the center. It works.

Same with thoughts. I try to think straight, but sometimes my thoughts lean to one side. **When my mind is missing the target, I aim it the other direction, to compensate.**

I tend to blame others too much. Everything bad is someone else's fault. So, to compensate, I assume absolutely everything is *my* fault.

I tend to underestimate how much time a project will take. So, to compensate, I make my best prediction, then *double* it.

I tend to assume I'm right. Then I noticed I was talking more than listening, and wasn't learning. So, to compensate, I assume I know *nothing* and have a lot to learn.

To be clear: The new thought is not meant to be correct. It's a counter-balance, to correct for my tendencies. Like aiming the bowling ball or frisbee to the right, so that it curves back into the target.

Another definition of the word "true" means straight and accurate. And the word "bias" means angled or curved. So we can choose beliefs that are not true because they're useful to compensate for our bias.

A DAILY RUN AND IMAGINATION

Every day you go for a run.

Sometimes you feel yourself lagging, so you imagine there's a tiger on your tail, and that adrenaline gives you a turbo boost.

Sometimes you feel like quitting, so you picture a pot of gold at the end, and that helps you finish.

A running expert says you should act like you're running on hot coals, to keep you on the front of your feet. You try it, and it improves your stamina and energy.

Sometimes, just for a change, you try running barefoot, or with your eyes closed, or with your arms out like an airplane. Every time you hear or think of a new way to run, you try it to see how it works and how you feel. The variety is fun.

All you changed was the image in your mind, and that changed your emotions and actions.

Ideas and beliefs are tools. Choose them for the desired effect.

Beliefs → emotions → actions

Let's look again at that example of the daily run.

If you believe there's danger right behind you, you'll feel scared and focus entirely on avoiding it.

If you believe there's a big reward at the end, you'll feel determined and push through your current pain — a small sacrifice for the eventual gain.

If you believe this is meant to be fun, you'll feel playful and find creative new ways to entertain yourself with no pressure.

Beliefs create emotions. Emotions create actions. **Choose a belief for the action it creates.**

Picturing one future makes you quit. Picturing another future makes you jump up, full of inspiration and action. A single thought can exhaust you or motivate you.

One thought makes you act selfish. Another makes you act generous. One thought makes you do something stupid. Another makes you do something smart.

Which belief is right? Wrong question. **Which belief leads to the action you need now?**

Useful?

Let's define "useful" as **whatever ultimately helps you do what you need to do, be who you want to be, or feel at peace**.

The word "ultimately" is there as a reminder of long-term consequences.

Is it more useful to make others see your point of view, or make yourself see theirs?

Is it more useful to think you're right, or to consider other perspectives?

Is it more useful to make your life easier, or make yourself stronger?

Is it ultimately more useful to benefit only yourself, or benefit others?

It depends on who you want to be and what helps you feel at peace.

Religion is action, not belief

One man believed God was on his side. He often lost his temper, hurt people, and did more harm than good. But he believed that what matters is what's in his heart, since God will forgive his actions and see his good intentions.

Another man was full of doubt but followed the rules of his religion. He stopped to pray five times a day, and donated to charity. He was calm and kind to everyone, no matter how he felt. He was never sure about his beliefs, but kept that to himself, since what mattered were his actions.

What is the point of beliefs if they don't shape your actions? It's easy to see the point of good actions without beliefs. It's easy to see which is better for the world.

Someone can practice a religion while questioning its beliefs, or believe its beliefs while not adhering to its practices. Notice the difference between religion and belief. Ideologies like capitalism, stoicism, and feminism are beliefs. Religions have behaviors, practices, and organization. Zen Buddhism is a religion with basically no beliefs.

There was no word for "religion" in most Asian, American, African, and Australian languages. The idea was introduced by Europeans. Before that, their word for spiritual practices was "law", "duty", "righteousness", or "the way". Even the Latin root of "religion" (religio) means "obligation". **Following a religion means doing, not just believing.**

Each religion is defined by its opposition. Protestants are not Catholics. Shias are not Sunnis. Christians, Muslims, and Jews are not pagans. Every religious believer knows other people believe something else. Therefore, no religion's beliefs are true, since conflicting beliefs exist. (Remember, "not true" does not mean false, but just not the only answer.)

But we can't say religions are not true, because that would be like saying dinner is not true. It's something you do. It's action and organization. Religion is not just in your mind.

People argue that their beliefs are true and other people's beliefs are false. But if they focus instead on the practices — the actions — they might find they actually have no problem with other people's religion.

Beliefs exist to guide your actions. If you're not acting in alignment with your beliefs, you've missed the point of beliefs.

Carpenters' tools

Two carpenters were fixing some stairs. The older one liked to work. The younger one liked to question.

The older one grabbed a measuring tape from the toolbox and started measuring. The younger one said, "What would be the perfect tool?"

The older one grabbed a saw and started cutting. The younger one said, "It would probably be a thick heavy level with a blade, ruler, chisel and saw, all built-in."

The older one grabbed a chisel and started fixing the edge. The younger one said, "Like a giant Swiss Army knife for professionals, to help us be really productive."

The older one grabbed a sanding block and finished the sanding. The younger one said, "That'd be so efficient, it'd be the only tool I'd ever need."

The job was finished, so the older one put away his tools and closed the toolbox to go. The younger one said, "Unless it would be smarter to just master the chisel, like a sculptor, right?" He kept talking as they left.

…

Some people want one perfect solution that solves every problem. They need everything to fit — consistent and congruent. The rest of us **use whatever tool helps us do what we need to do**. When someone refuses to use a tool because it's not perfect, they're probably not actually doing the work.

Judge the contents, not the box

My cousin took a course on a complete system for physical fitness and health, and followed every bit of its advice. She had great results at first. But then she saw the coach's social media posts, and hated his political beliefs, so now she doesn't follow that course at all.

A best-selling book on psychology is filled with wisdom that would improve your life, if applied. But a few sentences were found to be plagiarized, or some of its studies don't replicate. So people trash the whole book and refuse to read it.

That's the problem with judging a box instead of its contents. It's seeking "true" instead of useful. When any aspect of a package is flawed, it no longer feels "true", so all of it is discarded. You lose all of the benefits.

Think of a famous person you despise, perhaps a politician or celebrity that represents everything wrong with the world. Now imagine hearing that person say something you really like. Hard to imagine, right? You've probably pre-decided that anything that comes out of that person's mouth is going to be bad. No matter what they say, you're against it, in advance. Judging someone as good or bad, instead of each individual idea as useful or not.

Listen to ideas, not their messenger. Focus on the contents, not the box. Avoid ideology.

You've probably heard the phrase, "Perfect is the enemy of good." Likewise: **True is the enemy of useful.**

Which perspective empowers you?

There was a famous man who did many great things. After he died, they told stories glorifying him, painting him as flawless. But one story said he was not as great as he seemed — saying he was actually very flawed.

A young boy really looked up to this hero. The glorifying stories inspired him by showing him a role model of greatness. The boy worked as hard as he could and held himself to that high standard every day. But when he heard the disparaging story, his pursuit was no longer wholehearted, and he became aimless.

A different boy never liked that famous man. The glorifying stories discouraged him because they set an impossible standard. So when he heard the disparaging story, he got inspired. "If that jerk can do it, anyone can." This mindset made him work harder than ever to surpass the great bastard.

The two boys are a metaphor for your own internal incentives. It applies to stories of all types. Are you more inspired to think you've arrived, or have a long way to go? Does it help you to believe people can or can't be trusted? Do you like to see your life as shaped by destiny or chance? **Which story helps you do what you need to do, be who you want to be, or feel at peace?**

You don't need to decide which one is right. You can use one meaning to get you out of bed, and another to sleep well at night. Which meaning leads to the actions you need now?

Magic mirror shows what you need to believe

In Harry Potter, there's a magic mirror that reflects the viewer's desire. What Harry sees in that mirror is very different than what Dumbledore or Ron sees, because their desires are all different.

Imagine if there was something similar that shows you what you most need to believe right now. **It shows proof to support whatever perspective would most benefit you.** Upon seeing it, you instantly believe it, internalize it, and act upon it.

Someone feeling sadly disconnected might see proof that they are loved.

Someone working hard to create something might see proof that people will like it.

Someone with a terminal illness might see proof of an afterlife with loved ones waiting — to feel joy in their final days, and no fear of death.

We don't have to imagine this magic device. We already do this in real life. We find proof to support whatever perspective we need to believe.

We don't have to argue what's in the magic mirror, which viewpoints are true or not, because everyone needs different beliefs for their different situations.

Placebo meanings

Jerusalem is one of my favorite places. I hope to live there some day. Whenever I visit, I meet people who say they moved there from across the world because of the power of that place. They all say "it has an energy" and "you can feel it", as if it's an objective fact.

I've been to Bethlehem, the Temple Mount, and walked the Via Dolorosa. I've touched the Wailing Wall and the stones that held up Jesus' cross. I find them fascinating, but still just rocks — rocks with lots of meaning to other people. I feel no special energy.

But yet, when I'm in London, Manhattan, or Los Angeles, I feel that power they describe. (Feel free to tease me for this.) These places charge me, inspire me, and have real effects on my actions, maybe because my heroes created their greatest works there. So the power comes not from the place itself, but the meaning we give it.

This applies to anything. **Meanings are entirely in your mind. But their effect on you is real.** Like a placebo. It actually works.

So the reverse applies as well. If a meaning is holding you back, you can actively doubt it, question it, and find evidence against it, to stop believing it. Then it loses its power.

LIFE IS _____

I was at a workshop, and right before dinner, the teacher wrote this on the whiteboard:

LIFE IS _____

He told us to think about what goes in the blank. He said that after dinner, he'd reveal the meaning of life.

At dinner, I was at a table with seven other people, each arguing about what should go in that blank. One said life is learning. One said life is memory, since if you can't remember your life, it's like it never happened. One said life is love — the most powerful emotion. One said life is giving. One nouveau Buddhist said life is suffering, repeating his recent lessons. One said life is choice, since our choices shape our life. One said life is time, since life is what we call the time between when we're born and when we die.

Each was arguing that their answer was definitely the right one. I'm usually talkative, but I stayed quiet and just listened. Because there were different valid perspectives, it seemed clear that none of these could be *the* answer.

Then I thought maybe there is no answer — there is no built-in meaning. Maybe life is like a blank canvas for everyone to project their own meaning into.

Oh! Maybe that's why the teacher wrote:
"LIFE IS _____". Maybe that's not a question!
Maybe "_____" is the answer.
Ooooh that's good. I like that a lot.

After dinner, yeah, my hunch was right — that's what the teacher intended. He pointed up and asked, "What's the meaning of this ceiling?" Someone said, "It provides shelter." Someone else said, "Safety. Structure." The teacher said, "Those are your meanings. The ceiling itself has no meaning. It's just a ceiling."

He asked everyone, "What does it mean that you're here today?" Someone said, "It means I'm trying to improve myself." Someone else said, "It means I'm committed." The teacher said, "Those are your meanings. Your presence here today has no inherent meaning."

Then he asked, "So what's the meaning of life?" This time people's answers were emphatic, each arguing for their favorite meaning. The teacher said, "Those are your meanings. Life itself has no meaning." Now people were upset, saying this whole workshop was a scam and they want their money back since they expected an answer.

But I like that "_____" answer a lot. Not just for the meaning of life, but for everything.

You love travelling. What does it mean? You must be running away from something? You're privileged? You're a curious soul, searching for answers? Nah. **Nothing has inherent meaning. Whatever meaning you project into it is your own.**

You were just thinking of your long-lost friend this morning, and then they contacted you for the first time in years. What does it mean? Our psychic connections bind us? Our souls are in sync? The universe is sending out energy waves that we can feel? I mean, if you like that idea, why not? If that makes life feel more special, more magical... If that makes you curious about the unseen forces all around us... If that makes you marvel and wonder, then maybe that meaning works for you. Great. Give that event that meaning. **That's coming from**

you. Though maybe you need to believe it's true to feel its magic power.

Meanings can help you feel your life is important, with a narrative and purpose. Meanings can help you make peace with events out of your control. Meanings can give you a reason to persist in difficult times. **But they're internal, not external.** They're yours, not others'.

Me? I like the "_____". I like the blank canvas. I love that nothing, in itself, has built-in meaning. I love the creative power of choosing my own.

Meanings are useful, not true.

What is "the truth" really for?

You don't want a drill. You want a hole in the wall. So what do you really want when you seek "the truth"?

You can gather raw facts, but there are infinite facts, so you select and filter and interpret them. Like cotton plants or sheep's wool, facts are processed before they're used. Is that seeking the truth? Or just material for a story?

Maybe you're preparing for arguments. You want facts as weapons to defend your viewpoint and attack theirs. Facts can win a battle but not a war.

Maybe you're making a big decision. You want to feel well-informed and certain. But that's an emotional state unrelated to the facts. You'll ignore a mountain of evidence if you hear one good story against it or just feel yourself leaning the other way. Most emotions can't be persuaded.

You need to feel good about your choices. Emotion decides. Facts rationalize. You'll find whatever truth is useful.

Ask yourself why you want the truth. **What do you plan to do with it?** What's the real outcome?

Philosophies are instruments

Los Angeles, 1952. Igor Stravinsky, the composer, was 70 years old, and rehearsing the orchestra.

A young girl who lived next to the orchestra hall snuck in through the back door to listen to the rehearsals. She watched the violins, cellos, flute, trumpet, clarinet, harp, percussion, and piano. She wondered which one should be her favorite. There were too many options. She needed to pick one. During a break, she got up the courage to ask the maestro.

Stravinsky's friend and writer Robert Craft was there, so that's why this moment is captured.

The young girl went up to Stravinsky and said, "Excuse me. Which of these instruments is the best one?" He was surprised and amused, and took the challenge.

He said, "You hear sounds, but I hear life. Every instrument is a philosophy. **Every philosophy is an instrument.**" She just looked at him, confused, so he continued.

"You could pick just one instrument, one philosophy. But wouldn't it be more interesting to play them all?"

The girl said, "What?!? How could I play them all?"

Stravinksy said, "Let's say, as a young woman, you go out into the world to meet new people, full of multiculturalism and humanism. You do something daring, filled with optimism. Then you start a family and have time for nothing but pragmatism. You lose a loved one and comfort yourself with stoicism. But it makes no sense, so you're drawn to existentialism. See? So many instruments!"

The girl said, "What if I want to pick just one?"

He said, "Most people do pick just one. They think their instrument is the best! Go ask anyone in this orchestra, and they'll give you indisputable proof why their instrument is better than all others. You'll never convince that cellist that the clarinet is better, so why try? **Just like religions, cultures, and philosophies**, right?"

There was a long pause. The girl said, "So, which do *you* think is the best?"

Stravinsky smiled and said, "Time."

"Time?"

"Time! I can separate the instruments with time. Or I can combine them at the same time. Different instruments for different times in the music. Different philosophies for different times in your life. You can play every instrument, and every philosophy, if you use time, and combine. Time itself is my favorite instrument."

The girl seemed satisfied, and walked back to the balcony to listen again.

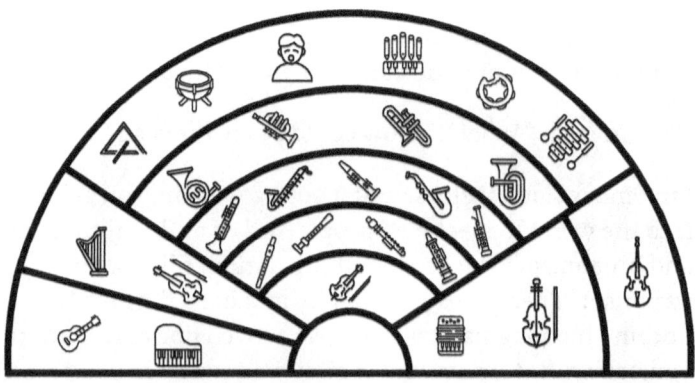

Reframe: Find Better Perspectives

The most useful part of this book

Imagine you're reframing a painting. First, you remove the old frame. Then you try different frames.

The first three parts of this book were helping you remove the old frame. That was just preparing for this. Now it's time to try different frames.

Explore many different ways of looking at your situation — finding perspectives you'd never considered before. Where you felt stuck, you'll see a great way out. You'll find an angle that excites you. What was cloudy will be clear plan of action. You'll see a smarter strategy. Where you felt haunted, you'll feel at peace.

These are the powers of reframing.

Who chooses your (next) thoughts?

You might say, "I can't help the way I feel", as if it's completely out of your control — as if you have no choice and are unable to feel any other way. But you do have a choice. Think a different way and you'll feel a different way. You choose your reaction. **Not the first one, but the next.**

There's a crucial moment in between when something happens and when you actually respond. It's an important life skill. It's as simple as this:

1. Something happens.
2. Get past your first emotional reaction.
3. Consider other ways of looking at it.
4. Pick one that feels empowering or useful.
5. It shapes how you feel and what you'll do.

Simple, but not easy. The hardest part was getting past your first reaction.

You choose how you think and feel. You choose your meanings. Other people's judgements, values, and meanings are also inside of you, but you can replace these with your own.

If you don't choose your perspectives then you leave them up to mood, manipulation, or your worst impulses. Control your thoughts or be controlled.

Answer great questions

Pick something that's holding you back from what you want to do, be, or feel.

It might feel like physical fact. "I'm too old." "I can't afford it." Even if you are old and have no money, that has not stopped others, so that's not the real problem.

Beliefs are often self-fulfilling. Whether you think you can or can't, you're right. Think nobody will love you? Think there are no opportunities? You can make bad dreams come true.

Doubt limitations. What's another way to see it? What perspective would help? Ask better questions.

"I'm too old" becomes "How can I use my age to my advantage?"

"I can't afford it" becomes "How can I afford it?"

Every problem becomes "What's great about this?"

Go back to your favorite books, movies, thinkers, or heroes. They're your favorites for good reason. They have lessons or wisdom you can use. What did they teach you? What would they say?

Ask any AI to list empowering questions. There's no shortage of great questions. But don't just ingest them. **You have to really answer them.**

Diamond in the trash

When things aren't going well, you're in a bad state of mind. If you ask yourself a healthy question, like "What's great about this?", your answer will probably be "Nothing! This is just bad!"

Don't be so sure. Push past that first thought. **Keep asking.** You can always find something useful.

Use what you learned about brainstorming. Don't stop at the second or third answer. Come up with crazy ideas.

Use what you learned from jigsaw puzzles. Start with the edges. Come up with extreme and ridiculous ideas that you'd never actually do, but are good for inspiration and finding the middle.

We resist good ideas that require us to change. You think you're not that kind of person? Not yet, but you can be. Keep all ideas around.

You *seem* to be locked in a jail cell. But if you *know* there's actually a secret exit, you'll look harder, pushing and pulling everything until you find it.

You *seem* to be holding a bag of trash. But if you *know* there's actually a diamond inside, you'll sift through the junk until you find it.

Your mind has a lot of trash, and often tells you there's no way out of your situation — there's nothing great about this. But if you *decide* that there is, you'll keep looking until you find it.

Expand your repertoire

To change, reach past what comes naturally. Avoid your defaults. Get guidance outside of yourself. Use a different tool.

"Oblique Strategies" is the name of a deck of cards where each card has one creative suggestion. When making music or anything, if you get stuck, you shuffle the cards, randomly pick one, and apply what it says. Some examples:

- Not building a wall; making a brick.
- Use an unacceptable color.
- Honour thy error as a hidden intention.

I had a poster on my wall of twenty different circles painted by twenty different artists. Each circle had a very different style, color, filling, and texture. When I didn't know what to do, I'd think how each artistic approach could be metaphorically applied to my life.

Now I learn about foreign cultures, and try to really understand the different worldviews. Instead of judging, I try to see the benefits of their perspective. I travel to inhabit philosophies.

In the spirit of all this, I wrote a book called "**How to Live**" that presents twenty-seven vastly different approaches to life, each taken to an extreme. It's meant to be used like the oblique strategies or the paintings of circles. I consider this book ("Useful Not True") to be like a prequel for that, so consider reading it next, in the mindset of reframing and finding other perspectives.

Traits of useful perspectives

To list all the beliefs I've found useful would fill a whole book. (Actually, four books so far, since that's what my previous books were about.) So instead, for your own ideation, it might help if I list the traits that my most useful perspectives have shared:

Direct: Go directly for what I really want, instead of using other means to get there. This requires soul-searching of my real motivations. What do I really want? And what's the point of that? Am I keeping a job just to feel secure? Getting a university degree for the status? Starting a business for the freedom? Instead, find a more efficient path to the real end result.

Energizing: I'll think of many smart but uninspiring perspectives, then one makes me bolt straight up in my seat, full of excitement. It inspires me to take immediate action. Note that fear is a form of excitement.

Self-reliant: It doesn't depend on anything out of my control. It doesn't need anyone's approval or involvement. It doesn't need anything to change. It works no matter what happens. It's about the process, not the outcome.

Balancing: Lately I've had too much of something, and not enough of something else. Comfort versus challenge. Social-time versus me-time. Exploring versus focusing. Prioritize what's been neglected.

Selfless: I see myself from the outside, and know that I basically don't matter. My needs are nothing compared to other people's, so how can I help? "Useful" means for them and the greater good.

Selfish: Generosity can go too far. Protect the goose that lays the golden eggs. Practice healthy self-respect and self-care that comes from self-worth.

Lucid and lasting: Coming from a good state of mind, not angry, hurt, envious, or upset — not even ecstatically happy. It's smart, and still seems like a good perspective a day or week later when I'm in a different state.

Test first: No matter how certain I feel, test an idea in reality. Before deciding, try it. Before buying something big, rent it, more than once. Before quitting, take a break.

Healthy: Do the right thing — do what's wise and good — even if I don't feel like it. Ask my idealized highest self how to think of this.

Long-term: In the big picture of my whole life, this is just a phase. Keep my eyes on the horizon. Short-term discomfort or pain can bring a deeply fulfilling reward. Serve the future.

Compensating for bias and prejudice: Correcting a bias, like my example of bowling and frisbee, earlier in this book. Do the opposite of my instincts. If I tend to walk away, I choose to stay. When I notice I'm prejudiced against something, I choose to get to know it and appreciate it. These have been the best beliefs for personal growth.

Five tiny tales of reframing

On the Olympic podium stood the winners of the gold, silver, and bronze medal. The silver medalist was so angry at herself for not being just a little bit faster — just milliseconds away from winning the gold. The bronze medalist was so happy with herself, just milliseconds away from winning nothing.

The former student was disheartened that she was failing at everything, so she went back to visit her old teacher. When she told him her troubles, the old man said, "Guess my secret number from 1 to 100."
"50?"
"Higher."
"75?"
"Lower."
With each try she smiled more, until she correctly guessed the number. Then she thanked him for the reminder that every wrong guess is not a failure, but just one step closer to success.

Two Japanese businessmen visiting Brazil had scheduled lunch to be delivered at 1pm. When the food finally arrived at 3pm, one of the men was furious. The other man was amused to witness this example of how differently their cultures treat time, and laughed at his own expectations.

A couple had been married for many years, but just divorced. The man's friends approached him with sad sensitivity, "Oooh. You must be devastated." But one friend greeted him with joy saying, "Congratulations! Nobody leaves a great relationship. I'm proud you both put an end to the struggle." This made him feel better for the first time.

How long should we mourn a loved one's death? For some people it's years or the rest of their life. But in a traditional New Orleans funeral, musicians accompany the coffin down the street, and after a few minutes of a solemn slow dirge, the music turns festive in a happy celebration. The funeral is a parade to honor that person's life, and the focus turns from grief to appreciation. Switching from sad to happy is always an option, even at the worst times in life.

An awesome collection of great questions

This is where I would share powerful questions that you can answer for big insights and change. But here's why I'm not:

I've read books that have long lists of questions. But when I'm reading, I want to keep reading, not stop for hours or days at that spot, pondering every question.

I've read books that act like a workbook, giving many blank pages with lines, expecting you to write your answers in that space. Does anyone actually do this? It doesn't work on the ebook or audiobook. I'd rather use my own journal.

If I put questions here, I'd think of better ones after the book is published.

So here's what we'll do: **Go to sive.rs/u**

That's the permanent website for this book, where I'll keep an ever-improving collection of helpful questions, free for you to take and use whenever you want. I hope you agree that it's better than this page of this book could ever be.

Adopt What Works For You Now

How to decide and make the best choice

You can do anything. But you can't do everything. You have to decide. If you don't decide, you get nothing.

You can think of a hundred paths to follow. But you can't follow them all. Use time. One path now. Other paths maybe later. Otherwise you'll never get anywhere.

How do you know what's the best choice? Trick question! **No choice is the best in itself. A choice becomes the best when you choose it.** That's when you make your decision congruent. You find plenty of proof to support it. Evidence against it is useless. You align yourself with your choice.

Best of all, you take action. By letting go of other options, you concentrate your energy and time. You make it part of your identity, and act accordingly. You become effective. You do the work that makes it a great choice.

From explorer to self-leader

Picture the stereotype of an explorer, hundreds of years ago, on an expedition to uncharted lands. The explorer tries everything. Up that river. Down that valley. Into every inlet. The explorer finds a nice harbor that would make a great port, and notifies the queen.

The queen appoints a captain to lead people to this new place. The leader is focused entirely on this destination. "Here's where we're going. Here's why. Here's how. Let's go." The leader describes the plan clearly and simply so it's easy to understand and repeat. The leader goes in a straight line, obstinate and undistracted. If a storm sends the ship off course, it gets back on course. If you tried to suggest, halfway there, "What if we tried somewhere else, instead?", the leader would ignore you.

This is a metaphor for two sides of yourself. When making a change in your life or your mind, you start by exploring. You take in tons of information, and keep searching for different perspectives.

Eventually, you don't need more information or time. You've found some good options. You need to decide. **You need to switch from explorer to leader — to leading yourself.** Stop considering other viewpoints. Stop changing the course. Pick a destination and cut off other options. "Here's where I'm going. Here's why. Here's how. Let's go." Describe the plan clearly and simply so it's easy to remember. Go in a straight line, obstinate and undistractable. Ignore that explorer inside of you that says, "What if I tried something else, instead?"

You can go back to exploring after you arrive at your destination.

No new instructions for the computer

You load the program into the computer, and it begins its calculations. It's computing. It's working hard, and it's going to take some time.

If you interrupt it with new instructions, it has to begin all over again, because the parameters have changed. **If you keep giving it new information, it will never finish its job.**

People who tell me they are lost and running in circles have one thing in common: They say they keep listening to podcasts, reading books, watching videos, doing courses — taking in more and more information — and still don't know what to do.

Consider the computer metaphor for yourself. You've taken in so much information, and heard so many instructions. That's enough input. It's time for output. Run the program. Stop interrupting yourself with new information. Let yourself execute one plan of action, and see it through to fruition.

Private journal to internalize it

Once you find a viewpoint you want to adopt, a great tool to internalize it is a private journal. Whether you write, type, or just talk, the point is to fill your mind with this new perspective.

Strengthen it by stacking up the reasons why you chose it.

"Here's how this will help me: _____"

"Here's how this will help others: _____"

Clarify it by defining it so simply that it's easy to remember.

"Here's how I'd explain it to a stranger in ten seconds: _____"

Plan it with a specific list of actions.

Picture the changes vividly. Describe your new self-identity and its implications.

Prepare for setbacks. Outsmart your future self that will try to revert to your old mindset. Trick the trickster in advance.

Come back and review your journal often, so you can remind yourself of your decision, reasons, vision, and plan.

Talk with friends to solidify it

After you privately internalize a belief, talk about it with friends. Explaining it to different people helps you refine it. They might see an angle or consequence you hadn't considered.

You hear it for the first time outside your own mind. You'll hear it sound wrong or right when telling someone else.

It feels like an announcement. It helps solidify the decision. You can ask them for help to support your choice, and to hold you to it.

We know ourselves through others. If people say you have nice eyes, then you must have nice eyes. When your friends acknowledge your belief and echo it back to you, it really feels like reality.

Why your choice is wrong

No matter what choice you make, someone will tell you it's wrong.

It's wrong because it's not what they would have chosen.

It's not what they need.

It's not the choice of other people they know.

It's not what an expert recommends.

The prosecution rests their case.

You might feel a need to defend it, or argue why you're right. Don't bother.

It's not for them, or anyone else. It's not even for your future or past. **It's only for you, and only for now.**

Your choice helps you do what you need to do, be who you want to be, or feel at peace.

It improves your current actions.

That's enough.

No need to argue that it's true.

Take the first step immediately

I spent basically my whole life in America, and had no desire to travel or be anywhere else. But one day I was thinking about growing older, and how people get stuck in their ways as they age. I thought what a learning experience it would be to move somewhere far away — somewhere that surprises me every day. Doing that often would be great for my brain.

The more I wrote about it in my journal, the more I felt it matched my values. So, out of curiosity, I looked up the price of a flight to London. It was only $400 round trip — a crazy sale price too good to miss. So without hesitation, I typed in my credit card and booked it.

It took a few seconds to realize what I'd done. I just committed to moving to London for six months. Whoa.

Four years later, I was living in Singapore, had a baby with a woman from India, and moved to New Zealand to raise him. I'm a citizen of three countries now, and deeply happy with my life. I think of the impact of impulsively booking that flight.

On the other hand, there were many times where I *thought* I wanted something — in theory — then took the first step, and realized I was wrong. **Taking action tests your thought in reality.**

Here's a good rule from experience: If you're considering something destructive — that would hurt someone or yourself — be very reluctant, keeping all other options in mind for some time. But for anything else, take the first step immediately, without hesitation. **Start momentum.**

Keep tuning and adjusting

When I got my first guitar, the nice man at the shop put on new strings and tuned it. A week later, I brought it back to the shop because it sounded terrible. He told me it was just out of tune. I said, "But you tuned it already!" He explained that I constantly have to re-tune it every time I play.

Same with adopting a new mindset. Every week, back in the journal, reflecting, talking with friends, and making adjustments.

Sometimes you need to stick to the plan exactly, and only adjust your thoughts. Sometimes you need to update the plan. Use your wisdom to decide.

Don't be discouraged when you get off course. A big benefit of keeping a journal is that you can **go back and review it**, to remind yourself what you're doing and why.

You are what you pretend to be

Your outside doesn't need to match your inside.

You can feel terrified inside, but just pretend to be brave for one minute. By doing that, you were actually brave.

You might be a total introvert, but need to attend an event, so you act social for one hour. By pretending to be social, you were.

You can imitate your role model. Many top performers have an alter ego — a Jekyll to their Hyde or vice-versa — a side of themselves they personify and bring out when needed. It's not Maria who negotiates. It's El Tigre.

I wasn't usually in the mood to be a good dad. But knowing how important it is, I'd collect my strength and do the right thing for a few minutes or hours — a short burst of being who my boy needed me to be. After years of that, we have an amazing relationship, and he tells everyone he has the best dad ever.

You are your actions. Your actions are you. Your self-image doesn't matter as much.

When you realize what you need to **do**, it doesn't mean that's who you need to **be**. You can just pretend.

AFTER

Reframing death

For the last three years, my boy and I have had a pet mouse. We got her from a pet store, and he's carried her in his hand through so many adventures in forests, beaches, and playgrounds. She sat on many little handmade boats down the creeks of New Zealand. Sand castles and Lego houses built just for her. Drawings and stories for and about her. You've never seen a mouse so loved.

The past six months, she's been next to me on my desk, twelve hours a day, as I wrote this book. Moving slower and wobbling, looking like she's in pain. This week, she kept falling over when trying to eat. Thirty minutes ago, she died. I'm surprised how much I've been crying.

As soon as she died, she looked at peace for the first time in months. It led to a thought that seems like a nice end to this book, and gives it extra meaning for me. Heaven is such a useful reframing. **Maybe it's the original reframing.** Death can be terrifying or devastating, so no wonder every culture found a way to reframe it.

Some people avoid loving pets or even people, because they're scared of the eventual heartbreak and loss. But avoiding sadness is like listening to music with only major chords. The minor chords are so beautiful. I'm crying, but isn't that wonderful? It's a part of a rich life.

And even *that* is reframing. It's a useful belief that has helped me love people and pets, again and again.

What next?

I have so much more to say on this subject, but this book is done now because I believe short books are useful. So the conversation continues on the website:

 sive.rs/u

There you will find more thoughts and stories around "Useful Not True". Please email me any questions or thoughts. I reply to every one. Go to:

 sive.rs/contact

To share my books with others, get them directly from me with quantity discounts, at:

 sivers.com

I hope you found this book useful, not true.

— Derek Sivers
New Zealand
July 2024 (Saturday, winter)

More books on this subject

Nothing and Everything by Val N. Tine
sive.rs/book/NihilismNE

Awaken the Giant Within by Tony Robbins
sive.rs/book/AwakenGiant

Useful Delusions by Shankar Vedantam
sive.rs/book/UsefulDelusions

Thinking in Bets by Annie Duke
sive.rs/book/ThinkingInBets

You Can Negotiate Anything by Herb Cohen
sive.rs/book/NegotiateAnything

The Courage to Be Disliked by Ichiro Kishimi and Fumitake Koga
sive.rs/book/Disliked

The Religious Case Against Belief by James P. Carse
sive.rs/book/AgainstBelief

How Religion Evolved by Robin Dunbar
sive.rs/book/ReligionHowEvolved

The Righteous Mind by Jonathan Haidt
sive.rs/book/RighteousMind

Sapiens by Yuval Noah Harari
sive.rs/book/Sapiens

Cows, Pigs, Wars, and Witches by Marvin Harris
sive.rs/book/CowsPigsWarsWitches

The Biggest Bluff by Maria Konnikova
sive.rs/book/BiggestBluff

How We Decide by Jonah Lehrer
sive.rs/book/HowWeDecide

Switch by Chip Heath and Dan Heath
sive.rs/book/Switch

 **The Happiness Hypothesis** by Jonathan Haidt
sive.rs/book/HappinessHypothesis

 **Pragmatism** by William James
sive.rs/book/PragWJames

 **Pragmatism an Introduction** by Michael Bacon
sive.rs/book/Pragmatism

 **Introducing Pragmatism** by Cornelis de Waal
sive.rs/book/PragmatismIntro

 **Pragmatism as a Way of Life** by Ruth Anna and Hilary Putnam
sive.rs/book/PragmatismWayOfLife

 **Delphi Complete Works of William James** by William James
sive.rs/book/WilliamJames

 **Philosophy: a Complete Introduction** by Sharon Kaye
sive.rs/book/PhilosophyCI

Cognitive Behavioral Therapy for Dummies by Rob Willson and Rhena Branch
sive.rs/book/CBDummies

The Philosophy of Cognitive-Behavioural Therapy by Donald Robertson
sive.rs/book/CBTphilo

The Alter Ego Effect by Todd Herman
sive.rs/book/AlterEgoEffect

How to Live by Sarah Bakewell
sive.rs/book/HowToLive

You Are Not So Smart by David McRaney
sive.rs/book/NotSoSmart

Overachievement by John Eliot
sive.rs/book/Overachievement

Scepticism: A Very Short Introduction by Duncan Pritchard
sive.rs/book/Scepticism

Being Logical: A Guide to Good Thinking by D.Q. McInerny
sive.rs/book/BeingLogical

Everything Is Obvious by Duncan Watts
sive.rs/book/EverythingObvious

Useful Belief by Chris Helder
sive.rs/book/UsefulBelief

Dreaming in Chinese by Deborah Fallows
sive.rs/book/DreamingInChinese

Loving What Is by Byron Katie
sive.rs/book/LovingWhatIs

Books by Derek Sivers

Anything You Want
40 lessons for a new kind of entrepreneur
sive.rs/a

Your Music and People
creative and considerate fame
sive.rs/m

Hell Yeah or No
what's worth doing
sive.rs/n

How to Live
27 conflicting answers and one weird conclusion
sive.rs/h

Useful Not True
sive.rs/u

www.ingramcontent.com/pod-product-compliance
Lightning Source LLC
Chambersburg PA
CBHW022020290426
44109CB00015B/1249